PEP TALKS

Answering Experience Questions

Dr. Jenice Armstead

Pep Talks

Answering Experience Questions

Copyright © 2013 By Jenice Renee Armstead

All rights reserved. No part of this document or the related files may be reproduced or transmitted in any form, by any means (electronic, photocopying, recording, or otherwise) without the prior written consent of the author

For More Information about the Author:
www.jenicearmstead.com

6" x 9" (15.24 x 22.86 cm)
Black & White on Cream paper
78 pages
ISBN-13: 978-1477511381 (CreateSpace-Assigned)
ISBN-10: 1477511385
BISAC: Business & Economics / Training

Pep Talks Series

Pep Talks: Answering Common Questions

Pep Talks: Answering Experience Questions

Pep Talks: Answering Past Employment Questions

Pep Talks: Answering Training Questions

Pep Talks: Answering The Hard Questions

Disclaimer

The reader should use their own judgment in utilizing the information in this book. The reader should seek advice from professionals as needed. The author's advice and information are based on professional experiences The author/publisher shall have neither responsibility nor liability to any person or entity with respect to any damages directly or indirectly as an aspect by any advice or information contained herein.

The author is not responsible for safety, wages, working conditions, or any other aspect of employment. All hiring, scheduling, and compensation are handled directly between the applicant and the employer.

Applicants are urged to perform due diligence when accepting, applying for, or interviewing with employers by requesting from each other references or any additional information needed to establish qualifications and credentials so as to ensure an overall fit between employer and applicant.

For additional information go to www.eeoc.gov

Biography

Dr. Jenice Armstead is a military veteran, author, motivational speaker, Professor and Academic Business Department Chair with over 17 years professional experience in the public and private sector. Jenice's expertise covers human resources, business management, the federal hiring process and government hiring policy. She understands the significance of human capital value for organizational development. She has an exceptional aptitude for teaching difficult topics with practical approaches. Jenice has a MBA with a Concentration in Human Resources from Saint Leo University and a Doctorate of Business Administration from Jones International University.

Dedication

To the job seeker, the economy would not exist without your passion for what you do. Press on toward your professional goals. Everyone needs a little "Pep Talk" every now and then. Stay motived and focused.

All the Best,
Dr. Jenice Armstead

Photo Credit: Robert Cass

Forward

The Pep Talks Book Series is an introduction to a new way of interviewing and obtaining a job in today's competitive market. The Pep Talks Book Series is all about giving the reader an advantage over their competitors when working toward the goal of gaining more knowledge and understanding in this new job market. This new job market is all about unconventional ways of obtaining knowledge while gaining the desired employment.

The Pep Talks Book Series explains how the new Job market knowledge and understanding how to better improve the chances of being "individually recognized" as a professional are vital.

The Pep Talks Book Series assists with building job confidence and self-esteem along with providing detailed examples for the reader to use for interviews.

The Pep Talks Book Series are designed to assist the reader in planning, executing, and managing their own career and potential growth in their field of choice.

Each section has an interactive "fill in the blank" area for guiding the reader with critical thinking activity examples to assist with brainstorming, and "Confidence Boosters" provide the reader with constant motivation for obtaining their "dream career."

The Pep Talks Book Series can serve the newly looking or the long-term job seeker with methods that will assist with the career search and provide motivation for future endeavors.

Pep Talks

Copyright © 2013 By Jenice Renee Armstead 2
Pep Talks Series 3
Disclaimer 5
Biography 6
Dedication 7
Forward 9
Overview 12
Introduction 14
YOU GOT THE INTERVIEW 23
   Pre-Interview Questions 25
      What will you wear? 25
      What will they ask? 27
      How early should I show up? 30
   Experience Questions 34
   What do you feel you can contribute to this organization? 38
      Confidence Boosting Affirmations 41
   What do you know about this Company? 43
      Confidence Boosting Affirmations 45
   What is your idea of the job you will be doing? ... 47
   What contribution do you think you can make to this company? 52
      Confidence Boosting Affirmations 55
   Why Are You Interested in this Job? 58
      Confidence Boosting Affirmations 61
   Conclusion 64
   References 66

Pep Talks
Answering Experience Questions

Overview

The Pep Talks Book Series clarifies difficult interview questions as the reader focuses on their goals. The Pep Talks Books Series gets the reader moving in the right direction, and saves the reader time and efforts, with helping the reader narrow down what areas they may need assistance with the most. The Pep Talks Book Series addresses all types of difficult interview questions that may be asked of the reader during an interview or during a conversation being had by an interviewer.

An interview can seemly happen at any given time, so it is good practice to have some "pre-set" answers to some of these questions. Nervousness often happens during interviews or with conversations with people whom are not familiar to the candidate.

The Pep Talks Book Series are designed to assist the reader in planning, executing, and managing career goals and potential growth in the field of choice. Each section has interactive "fill in the blank" area for guiding you with critical thinking examples to assist with brainstorming and "Confidence Boosters" provide you with constant motivation for obtaining your "dream career."

The Pep Talks Book Series can serve the newly looking or the long-term job seeker with methods that will assist with the career search and provide motivation for future endeavors.

Introduction

Are you looking for more interview guidance that will actually work and get you that job? If so, then you have come to the right place. You are here because you want an unconventional way of motivating, obtaining and sustaining your career goals.

There are a few key items that must be taken into careful thought. It is important to realize that in today's job market you must have some type of people skills. People skills can make or break any job opportunity you could have. In today's job market, you must be a "Jane or Jack" of all trades, this includes being "approachable" and potentially "likeable." You must know how to have a conversation with just about anyone, at just about any time at any place.

The truth of the matter, is that today's job market is full of unconventional opportunities. The opportunities are truly everywhere. You are your own "Sales Person." If you have never been in sales, you are now. When you are marketing yourself to employers, you must "sell" your skills. You must be ready for any type of interview, at all times. You have to be personable, approachable and presentable at all times. Being mindful of your language, dress and even your hairstyles. These are important facets of the entire interviewing process when looking for employment.

Conversations are a key element to obtaining jobs. Small talk must be utilized and practiced. Employers are looking for people they connect with and ultimately trust. Eye contact is crucial, if you have trouble-keeping eye contact – practice in a mirror. You must know how to have a conversation with just about anyone, at just about any time, or anywhere. Opportunities knock when you least expect it, so you need to be ready to answer the door at any time of day, or night.

When I say you have to be ready at all times, I mean at ALL times. For example, while shopping for groceries in a super market you could be approached by a random person that strikes up small talk with you, and before you know it you find yourself in a "mini interview" situation. "How so?" you ask. Well, if you are looking for employment, you should state it in the conversation when ever possible. Conversations are essentially "mini interviews." If anything, you can use the opportunity as practice to get confortable with small talk and eye contact.

You could even have a small conversation with someone at a gas station. "Gas station!?" You ask? I say with great positive affirmation, YES! You could have a "mini interview" even at a gas station. Managers and recruiters are everywhere.

When I say "affirmation, if you are not familiar with positive affirmations, these are your own personal slogans you use to keep yourself positive, uplifted, motivated and focused on your overall goal. I often use affirmations, so I decided to include them in the Pep Talk Book Series. Affirmations are found through out this book. Affirmations are known to work. Having positive talks with yourself keep you uplifted, motivated, and ensure you are "checking in" with yourself on a higher level of positive awareness.

It is also a good practice to keep business cards and resumes with you at all times. If you don't have business cards, get some! They are fairly inexpensive and you could make them yourself, or purchase them in bulk for a fairly reasonable price. A business card says a lot about yourself when you meet a potential employer. Be mindful of the colors and font choice on the business card. You want to make sure you are using neutral colors and a large enough font to be viewed by anyone. Keep it simple; include your name, your email address, a slogan or motto. Include your point of contact phone number. Remember, business cards are used as "point of contact cards," not resumes.

Don't over load business cards with your entire resume or all the jobs you have ever had. Make sure to add your email or website on the back. Have you noticed that when you give a business card out to someone, they immediately look on the back while you are chatting with them? This is because they are looking to see if you took the time to put anything on the back. Why wouldn't you put something on the back? If you don't, it is left blank. This is a missed opportunity. Make sure you put something on the back of your business card. At the minimum, put your name and email on the back. This ensures that even if your business card is face down, you are still "there and relevant." It is important to stay relevant to employers.

A quick story, I was on my way home from a job interview I had just finished up. I was feeling great about myself and was taking audio notes in my car on my cell phone. While getting out of my car a woman stopped me and asked if I knew of any good places to eat. I greeted her with a huge smile and mentioned a few places in the neighborhood. She then informed me that she was in town for a business convention. After some small talk about her business, she told me that she was a human resources professional and her assistant fell ill and was unable to assist her with her booth. I handed her my business card and she looked to the back and saw my slogan "Opportunity is Everything." She smiled and I knew I had immediately impressed her.

I told her a little bit about myself and she offered for me to be her assistant for the day. I was excited, and calmly replied with a "of course I will be your assistant for the day." Long story short, she happened to be the Human Resources Director of her company. Even though it was only a day job, it was a networking opportunity that completely out weighted the pay being offered.

This is just one example of how people skills and opportunities merge into great professional ventures. You, the job seeker, must be ready for any type of interview, or opportunity at all times. You have to be personable, approachable and presentable at all times. When I say all times, I mean at ALL times.

It is a good practice to keep business cards and resumes with you at all times. I don't know how many times I have asked someone for their contact information and they scramble for a piece of paper. It is important to have business cards on you at all times, I have business cards for just about everything, including when I meet a new friend and want to exchange information with them. You must always be ready for the unexpected interview or networking opportunity anywhere, with anyone and in any situation at all times. This is one of the reasons why I have created these easy to use and follow booklets.

With the Pep Talks Book Series, you can be ready at all times. With helpful insight, interview tips and advice, examples and interactive questions to help with the interview process toward getting the position that you have been dreaming of. You have just opened "unseen" doors for yourself, and your interviewing skill sets will improve with using the Pep Talks Book Series.

YOU GOT THE INTERVIEW

Long hours of filling out applications and attaching resumes have finally provided you with an interview. You have finally received that phone call or email that you have been waiting for. You got your call back and now it is time for one of the most important days of your career, the interview. Now it is time for you to shine, but like all professional events, you need to practice first.

Now comes the hard part, the job interview process. There are a few questions that you may have even before you can start to smile about having the interview. What will you wear? What will they ask? How early is too early to show up for an interview?

These are all legitimate questions to think about and ask. Remember, it is never too early to start practicing and preparing for an interview. Keeping a positive attitude about getting an interview is just as important as keeping a even more positive attitude during the interview process. You only get one chance for a first impression. The Pep Talks Book Series will ease some of the stress you may have, so let's get started!

Pre-Interview Questions

What will you wear?

You are going to want to wear the best business attire that you have. It is important not to wear all black or all blue. Make sure to keep your attire in the "neutral" colors such as brown, black, blue and tan, but mix and match the colors to look professional.

Be sure to wear a combination of these colors in your attire if you can. An eye-catching attire would be if you wore a brown suit with a blue shirt or blouse under your suit jacket. This allows you to stand out and be remembered, you want the interview panel to remember you and your professional attire. Either way, this will make you look not only professional and well put together, but you will be able to show off your professional personality as well.

Professional personality involves some serious thought. No florescent, no 3-inch heels, no big chunking or dangly jewelry and no heavy perfumes. All of those items will take away from the fact that you are there for an interview and you want to be taken seriously. You are not there to make a fashion statement, but to show the interviewer that you are a true professional in every sense of the word.

Believe it or not, all of the items I have listed are not only distractions to the interviewers but they can be taken as professionally disrespectful. No one is saying that you have to dress with no style or pizazz. Dress professionally appropriate for the position for which you are interviewing. You will be glad that you listened! Believe me.

What will they ask?

Preparing for an interview is a daunting task if you have no idea what will be asked of you during the interview. But you can have some pre-set answers to questions that may be asked of you. Make sure to practice a combination of questions that could be asked of you. You can be sure that during any interview you will be asked about yourself, your experience and your education or on-the-job training. These are some points that will be addressed at some point in the interview.

Remember to "actively" listen to the questions that are being asked of you during the interview, you may find that the pre-set answers that you have rehearsed may need to be instantly edited during the interview process. Not to worry, because practice makes perfect – you will know when to instantly edit the answers and when to just use the pre-set answer you have practiced.

Active listen skills are important. Most people don't use "active" listening skills. If you are in a conversation just waiting to spew your opinion or response, you are not using your "active" listening skills.

Actively listening, means to really take in and digest the information coming from the other person's words, hear what they are saying and think about what they are saying before you respond. You can easily practice this in your everyday life. With your friends, family and in day-to-day conversations with random people you meet.

The key to "active" listening is to being present in the moment the other person is speaking, taking it in and understanding the feeling they are having during the conversation. It takes practice and time, but it is a valued skill set.

Although, there is no way to fully prepare for any specific interview, there are a few key points to remember are 1) always give a firm hand shake, 2) Make sure to keep smiling and 3) be presentable. Implementing these 3 simple key points and preparations will allow for interview to go smoothing.

 A firm handshake is one of the simplest ways to establish confidence before an interview. The interviewer or panel analyzes a handshake. If a handshake is weak, flimsy or sweaty, this could give off the wrong impression about you. A weak handshake could say that you are intimidated. A flimsy handshake could say that you really don't care to be at the interview, and a sweaty handshake could say that you are extremely nervous.

 A smile is worth a thousand words. Smiling during the pre-interview or introductions give the interviewer the insight that you are happy to be there, or that you are feeling confident about having the interview. No matter how you are feeling about the interview, a smile is always a key element.

Being presentable is a necessity. There have been times where candidates did not take the needed time to look appropriate, and managers have excused the candidate to not be apart of the selection process. It doesn't matter if you have the most experience or education, being presentable is a must. This includes removing any piercings, pulling hair up in a neat bun or out of your face and ensuring you don't have body odor.

How early should I show up?

During in initial interview, it is good practice to give yourself at least 15 to 20 minutes leeway to get to your interview on time, find a parking place and time to find the building or suite of the office you're looking for. It is a good practice to keep in mind traffic, and uncontrolled situations that may be out of your control while driving. If you live in a more congested area, allow for additional time. Remember it is always better to be too early than late. If you arrive more than 20 minutes, at least you are there and can wait in your car or at a local coffee shop until your interview time is scheduled.

If you are driving, fill your gas tank up the night or day before your interview. Situations have been known to happen to interviewees at gas stations that can cause significant delays for arriving on time to an interview.

For example, there is a gas leak, which can make you late, you may get gas on your outfit, which makes you smell of gas or getting gas merely makes you late because of traffic.

Either way, all of these situations are possibilities to actually happen. I know, they have happened to me right before an interview. The last thing you want to do is come to an interview late with some kind of "dog ate my homework" excuse. This will only give the interviewer a misconception about your lack of professionalism that may not be true.

These are only a few question examples that will be discussed in the "Pep Talks Book Series" which will assist with interviewing dilemmas.

These sample questions and answers will give you a "leg up" on your peers and will assist with making you look and sound like the "best candidate" for the job.

Practicing with others for feedback is a great way to see how your skills have improved over time. Like any other skill, interviewing takes time and effort to find what works for you. You have what it takes, and with a support system your dream job or career is within your reach. Don't forget to practice your questions in the mirror with yourself, and record yourself to improve upon your interviewing skills.

Many people don't realize how often they

"break" eye contact during a conversation. Eye contact is important at all times. Many employers have been known to NOT hire a candidate based on a lack of eye contact.

Practicing in a mirror, with friends and with people that you randomly meet will assist with development a comfort with keeping eye contact with people.

Are you ready to boost your confidence and stay motivated toward obtaining your dream career – if so, let's continue on with "Answering Experience Questions" that could be asked of you during your interview. Believe in yourself, and your abilities, because – **I BELIEVE IN YOU** ☺! It is now time to get your PEP TALK!

Experience Questions

Interviewing can be nerve shattering and can take a toll on your emotions. The best way to make sure you do your best during ALL interviews is to practice, practice, and practice. Interviewing is a skill set like any other skill. It must be practiced in order to develop a natural flow. To improve upon your skills you must practice. Practice interviewing with others, yourself and always continue to improve your skills by recording yourself as you are practicing. Recording yourself allows for you to reflect on where you can develop your skills. Your interviewing skills will set you apart from other candidates, be confident in your skills.

The reassuring part about answering experience questions is that there is no way in the world that a peer candidate will have your exact job experience, unless they have worked at every single job and position you have – which is very unlikely.

Experience interview questions are an excellent way for you to show off your outstanding job ethic and working experience. There are many experience questions that could be asked of you, and your job during the interview process is to be confident, honest and as open as possible about your experience. Give examples of your experience, make the interviewer interested in what you have done and accomplished. This is your opportunity to "brag" about what you have done for other companies or organizations.

Experience questions "test" the interviewees' personality, speak about your previous positions and experience with positive tones and confidence. Showing that you are positive and confident will affirm to the interviewer that you enjoy what you have done in the past.

Most experience questions are asked for the interview panel to see how you work in stressful work situations, how well you work in teams and how you respond to difficult situations.

Take some time to write down some key events that you did or completed at previous jobs that were unique to you and your abilities. Start with making a list of professional accomplishments, then continue with a list of projects and goals that you accomplished.

Experience questions will show the interview panel why your experience makes you a true professional, and confident in what you have done.

Here are the questions that will be addressed:
- **Why do you feel you can contribute to this organization?**
- **What do you know about this company?**

- What is your idea of the job you will be doing?
- What contribution do you think you can make to this company?
- Why Are You Interested in this Job?

Let's look at each of these 5 Experience Interview questions, you could be asked. More than likely you could be asked at least one of these questions during your interview. But, don't worry by the time you finish reading this booklet, your skill set for answering experience questions will be stronger.

YOU CAN DO IT! ☺

What do you feel you can contribute to this organization?

When answering work experience questions, it is important to be professional and honest about previous work completed. Many work experience interview questions relate to interest in the job, contributions to the previous held positions, and or what a previous employer may or may not say about your work ethic.

Many aspects of your life will come up in any length of a job interview. One of those aspects that may be asked about is your professional goals and your contributions to a possible position or company. Keep in mind that when going on a job interview, one needs to act as though they are going to start the position that day.

This means that all questions must be answered with confidence and affirmation of positive thoughts of already having the position you are interviewing for. This brings you to the question at hand. The way this interview question could be answered has many facets to it.

RESPONSE INTERACTIVE EXAMPLE

"I feel that I can contribute to this organization because I am skilled in

_____

_____
and_____

_____.
I also have specialized experience in _____

_____

_____. I am able to handle highly stressful work situations, being that I have worked in_____
field for a_____
(months/years)."

First, have a quick idea of what your attributes are. Go to your notes if need be. After a few seconds, state all the good things you bring to the position including the ability to handle high stressful situations. After you state some general positive contributions you bring to the organization, state some direct contributions you bring to the organization.

Make sure to use terminology directly attainable toward the position you are interviewing for. This is a difficult interview question to answer, but if you come professionally and mentally prepared you are sure to impress the interview panel or manager; as well as to show how competent you are. You will be sure to reaffirm the interviewer of your professional abilities and leave a lasting impression, which will be sure to set you above all the other candidates.

Confidence Boosting Affirmations

- ✓ I am a attribute that this organization needs
- ✓ I show my professional worth at all times
- ✓ I answer all interview questions with confidence
- ✓ I have vital professional attributes
- ✓ I know this organization needs my knowledge and skills
- ✓ I have the courage to speak with confidence
- ✓ I concentration on my key priorities
- ✓ I am professional at all times
- ✓ I remain focused and motivated
- ✓ I am _____
- ✓ I am _____
- ✓ I am _____

Interview Preparation Notes

What do you know about this Company?

This is a question that normally gets asked in the beginning of the interview. Recalling when this question has been asked of myself, it is important for you to be honest. If you don't know anything about the company then say so, but then follow up with something to the manner of wanting to know more about the company. If you know absolutely anything of the company you can use what you do know about the field of work you are interviewing for as a "save" to still answer this question fully.

If you come across a situation such as this, don't try to "pretend" that you know the answer if you haven't done the necessary research. A recommendation to do some research on the company is always a good one.

RESPONSE INTERACTIVE EXAMPLE

"I haven't had a chance to research this company, but I do know that _____ is a growing field. I have a willing to learn more about the company, the mission statement and how the company could use my skills."

Or

"No, I can't say that I am familiar with this company, but what interested me was the job announcement and job description. Could you possibility tell me a little bit about the company?"

    The reason it is important to be as honest as possible is because if you state that you do know about the company, you will probably be asked what you know about the company. Then you would be caught in a situation where you were found to be dishonest.

The last thing you want to do is say you know something and you don't. The interviewer will then question everything about your interview, including your job experience and resume information.

Confidence Boosting Affirmations
- ✓ I am able to speak about myself with ease
- ✓ I am an approachable and well spoken
- ✓ I look people in the eyes with ease
- ✓ I am a creative person with professional attributes
- ✓ I am an honest, loyal and peaceful person
- ✓ I deserve success and happiness
- ✓ I am open to having a successful career
- ✓ I have endless supplies of motivation and energy

Interview Preparation Notes

What is your idea of the job you will be doing?

This question shows what kind of thought you have put into understanding the position, which has been applied for. It is good practice to do a bit of research on the company, the company's competitors, and position that you are interviewing for before you go to the interview.

With this particular interview question it is important to have an idea of what the position entails and what the job description is, this gives you an idea of what the position will be about. Reading the job description may be a bit confusing, so it is recommended to research some similar positions and compare the position descriptions to that of the one you will be interviewing for.

In many cases, the position descriptions for most jobs can be found on a website: www.onetonline.org. This website is an excellent source for reading position descriptions and gaining a better idea of other duties could be entailed in the position you are applying for.

Start off by talking about what the job announcement you applied for stated, then continue with what you believe the job is about using the knowledge you gathered from your previous research.

This will show how serious you are about obtaining the position, which you are interviewing for. You will not only impress the interviewer, but this will be something that will give you a few bonus points or taking extra time for preparing for the interview.

RESPONSE INTERACTIVE EXAMPLE

"I feel that the position I applied for is for a _____

_____

_____. I have read the job description

for the position and the overall thought with the job duties include _____

_____ and

_____

_____. I have specialized knowledge in

_____

_____

_____. Is there anything else you can elaborate on with what other duties or responsibilities the job will entail?"

Or

"I read the job description and I have an idea of what the job would entail, but I would appreciate any additional information you could provide about the duties of the job."

Confidence Boosting Affirmations

- ✓ I know what the job is and what will be required of it
- ✓ I understand the organizations mission statement
- ✓ I am a perfect fit for the job I am interviewing for
- ✓ I am the best candidate for this position
- ✓ I have patience with the interviewing process
- ✓ I am proud of myself
- ✓ I have control of my behavior at all times
- ✓ I am happy with my life
- ✓ I allow for healthy business opportunities to come to me
- ✓ I gratefully accept goodness and happiness in my life
- ✓ I choose to focus on thoughts that uplift my purpose

Interview Preparation Notes

What contribution do you think you can make to this company?

During an interview it is important to display the contributions that you as the candidate may bring to the company. In this time in our economy an interview is more than just that, it is also an opportunity for networking. Networking is a huge part of the interviewing process. Even if you are not selected for the positions, other opportunities could be had because of something you may have mentioned.

During an interview I had when I was younger, I was asked to talk about my contributions in my past positions. I spoke of working in the military and with higher-ranking officials. Long story short, I didn't get the job, but I did get a temporary job opportunity that turned into a permanent position. This is why it is important to stay open and positive during the interview process.

Contributions are an excellent way for you to stand out during a job interview. When asked this question, it is important to start your reply off with something that is centered on what you will bring to make the company better.

Say you are interviewing for an administrative position. You could state your diverse ability to work with different types of software to organize work flow to be more productive in getting the mission of the company done at a faster pace. This is great contribution to mention. You are able to show your knowledge, skill sets and abilities.

RESPONSE INTERACTIVE EXAMPLE

"I would bring an expert knowledge in the field of
_____
_____
_____
_____and
_____
_____.

I also bring experience in the background of a vast array of software's such as _____
_____
_____
_____
_____
_____
_____.

     You could also answer directly, by stating something to the angle of being more organized and implementing your organizational ability toward the position. Either way, it is important to explain in great detail how you will be a positive contributor to the company. If you are worried about not remembering everything, you could write your bullets down to refresh your memory before the interview.

Confidence Boosting Affirmations

- ✓ I bring expert knowledge that this company needs
- ✓ I am a subject matter expert in my professional field
- ✓ I have what it takes to show that I have expert knowledge
- ✓ I am increasing my professional knowledge everyday
- ✓ I am always ready for opportunities at all times
- ✓ I am fully focused and present

Interview Preparation Notes

Why Are You Interested in this Job?

Whether your reasons for the position are financial gain or relocation, it is important to know that this interview question is one of the most standard questions asked in almost every interview. Job interest is equivocated to professional goals. This is a question that needs to be fully thought about before one goes into a job interview. This question should be answered in the sense of what the job is and the interests of the interviewee.

The fact that the job may deal with working with contracts and acquisitions, or the fact that the job allows for exposer to needy people with the ability to challenge oneself in certain situations.

When answering this question it is vital to keep to the facts of the job description and what the job actually entails. An easy way to know if the perspective of the job is right is by reiteration of what you believe the position is about.

This also shows the interviewer or panel that you have a full understanding of the job description and what the job duties. In some cases, interview panels have been prone to making final selections based on how this question is answered. This is another one of those "honesty" questions. Interviewers know if you are giving a "text book" answer, or if you are being genuine about answering this question. The key to answering this question is to give a blended answer with both the facts and a creative response with why you are interested in the position.

RESPONSE INTERACTIVE EXAMPLE

"There are many reasons why I was attracted to and interested in this position. The first reason was the position seemed to jump out at me and the pay was attractive. I do feel that I am a great fit for this position because of my background being directly related to all of the information in the job announcement."

Or

"I am in interested in this position because it is what I have been looking for in growth for myself in my field, I am a true professional and know that being selected for this position would be a great fit for both the company and myself."

Or

"I am interested in the company and the position for a number of reasons starting with_____

_____.

No matter what you say, make sure to keep eye contact and speak with confidence about your reasons. If you are interested in the salary, state that. If you are interested in the location, state that. If you are interested in the benefits package, state that. Stating all of these things will bring up more questions for interviewers to ask, and the more clarification you have, the better. Remember, you are in an interview, but they are being interviewed for your acceptance if you choose to accept the position as well.

Confidence Boosting Affirmations

- ✓ I have a full understand what is required of the position
- ✓ I am the perfect fit for this position
- ✓ I am the best candidate for this position
- ✓ I am a hard worker and my experience show it
- ✓ I am able to remove all nerviness and be professional
- ✓ I accomplish more each and every day
- ✓ I am thankful for the opportunities presented to me

Interview Preparation Notes

Conclusion

Applying for a job can be stressful, but at the same time the interviewing process can be even more stressful. Make sure you are prepared for any question that may be asked of you.

You have the right to not answer inappropriate or unethical interview questions. Remember that any questions dealing with sexuality, religion and political party preference or any other topics are not allowed to be discussed. Under the Equal Opportunity Employment Commission (EEOC) are questions that should not be asked during any interview. For more information go to www.eeoc.gov.

As an applicant you have the right to choose to not answer the question or leave an interview at any time and report unlawful behavior to the EEOC.

You are motivated to walk into any job interview and obtain your position/job of choice. Take this booklet with you if you need any refreshers before your interview and make sure to complete all the exercises.

Remember, PRACTICE, PRACTICE, and more PRACTICE makes you a perfect interviewee. But remember, everyone needs a little "Pep Talk" every now and then, YOU CAN DO IT! I believe in you and now, believe in yourself and get your dream job!

All the Best,
Dr. Jenice Armstead, United States Navy Veteran

References

Armstead, J. (2010). Retrieved May 2, 2010, from http://jenicearmstead.com/

About the EEOC: Overview. (n.d.). US EEOC Home Page. Retrieved August 12, 2012, from http://www.eeoc.gov/eeoc/

Jackson , Oscar. "Developing and Administrating Structured Interviews." Personnel Assessment Division. Office of Personnel Management. US Government, Washington, DC. 2001. Reading.

Other Books by Dr. Jenice Armstead

Dr. Jenice Armstead has self-published several books to include: business, self-improvement and healthy cooking books.

You can find all of these books on the official website www.jenicearmstead.com